TALES FROM THE CHEROKEE HILLS

TALES FROM
THE CHEROKEE HILLS

JEAN STARR

John F. Blair, Publisher
Winston-Salem, North Carolina

Cover illustration, "Firebringer" by Shan Goshorn
Book design by Debra L. Hampton
Typesetting by Superior Typesetters, Winston-Salem, North Carolina
Printed by BookCrafters, Chelsea, Michigan

Library of Congress Cataloging-in-Publication Data

Starr, Jean.
Tales from the Cherokee hills.

1. Cherokee Indians—Poetry. I. Title.
PS3569.T336228T35   1988   811'.54   88-14655
ISBN 0-89587-062-2

To my father,
   who taught me to tell stories,

to Walter Van Tilburg Clark,
   who taught me how to write,

to John Fries Blair,
   who chose to publish this book,

and to my husband, Winn Starr,
   who helps me with everything,
   especially the parts that come out right.

Contents

Foreword

It is always a delightful experience to read the works of a Cherokee writer that transcend the generations. I found the stories included in this collection hauntingly familiar, like those I heard as a child. Telling stories has always been part of the oral tradition of the Cherokee people. That Jean Starr has chosen to put them in written form is a tribute to the past values that need to be preserved for present and future generations.

I especially appreciated the warmth and humor in which the stories were related. The depth of meaning did not escape me. I always appreciate the writing of those who perceive more than one reality.

Wilma P. Mankiller
Principal Chief
Cherokee Nation of Oklahoma

Acknowledgment

Loretta Shade of the Cherokee Cross-Cultural Center in Tahlequah, Oklahoma, served as consultant on the translation and transliteration of the story titles into the Cherokee language.

Introduction

Many people read American Indian folklore anticipating stories of interest mainly to children, looking for neat parallels to Cinderella and Rapunzel. Like fairy tales, Indian stories are intended to teach, but they are also designed for presentation to a wide variety of ages at a single telling. They have multiple layers of meaning, and they are meant to give listeners new insights and to effect change in them. In their attempt to explain the world, Indian stories comment on the human condition and give examples of how to live and how not to live. But at the same time, they are intended to entertain.

I was raised among storytellers. My father could turn almost anything into a funny or frightening tale. His repertoire featured tales of disappearances in the woods, hunters pursued by wild animals, and mysterious lights and noises deep in the forest. Other relatives and friends were notable storytellers, too. Their best efforts were reserved for dark, windy nights with rain drumming on the galvanized roofs, or for nights in the woods around a fire.

For the modern reader, and the non-Indian reader in particular, gaining an understanding of these stories is not the simple task it was for the family members and friends who gathered around the fire when they were originally told. There are linguistic and cultural barriers to overcome, and great barriers of time and space as well.

Like most Indian people, Cherokees have an acute sense of humor. Cherokee is very much a punster's language, in which it is impossible to avoid double meanings. The traditional personal names are formed from common nouns—Frog, Beaver, Beans—which are, in turn, formed from verbs. For example, Siquaujesdi, meaning Possum, is a common name derived from "He laughs."

Cultural obstacles must also be overcome if these tales are to be properly appreciated. The story that ends this book concerns a girl who can't cook. The point of the story is that every girl was expected to cook, to cook well, and to be able to cook kanuche, the dish that is the center of contention. It's important to know that a Cherokee girl who has no notion of how to make kanuche is the equivalent of an American boy who looks at a baseball bat and asks, "What's that?" I've always thought that the girl in the story is only pretending not to be able to cook, and that's why I've written two versions of the tale. In this case, and in many others, ambiguity is intended by the storyteller.

The essence of life as these stories depict it is not ambiguity, but mystery. When the Cherokee traditionalists get up before first light to greet the dawn, they are expressing a personal religious act and a complicated attitude toward the central mysteries of life. Today, we are taught to be reluctant to acknowledge the limits of human understanding. Things we do not understand fill us with terror, and we want to believe that nothing is beyond our control, that nothing can surprise us. A Cherokee's hymn to the dawn seems alien, whether it is viewed as an emotional response, an aesthetic response, or a religious response. But scientific descriptions of the dawn fail to convey a sense of beauty, awe, and fear. Traditional Cherokee stories usually begin with the words, "It was amazing . . ."

In the Cherokee tradition, there is a Creator-God who is benevolent and omnipotent. The Creator can manifest himself in other forms with lesser abilities.

Humans are endowed with a certain potential, and spiritual fulfillment centers on the recognition and achievement of this potential. When undertaking a task—

whether growing crops, producing a work of art, or striving at any other important endeavor—it is necessary to call on energies beyond one's own, just as it is sometimes necessary to call on other energies in times of danger. The person who is most in harmony with his or her environment, including other humans, is best able to use these energies. It is this harmony, or Orinda, that is the aim of Cherokee spiritual life. Hatred, anger, resentment, and other negative feelings make it impossible to achieve the Orinda, as does any kind of excess, particularly excessive emotion. Harmony with people requires both the willingness to forgive and the ability to accept forgiveness. Harmony with the inanimate world goes something like this: one's bones are like the rocks of the earth, one's flesh is like the dirt to which it will someday decay, and one's veins are like the streams of the earth.

The setting depicted in these stories is as different from modern urban life as the belief system just described is from contemporary values. Villages typically contained between five hundred and a thousand people. They were located on a creek or small river near a forest; usually, a small stream running through the village provided both a water supply and a fish pond. Fields were cleared from the forest for the cultivation of corn, beans, tomatoes, potatoes, sweet potatoes, squash, peppers, and pumpkins. Underbrush was cleared up to the town wall, a log palisade some ten or twelve feet high.

Houses were constructed of woven withes plastered smoothly with daub, forerunners of the log cabins of the pioneers. They were used primarily for storage, sleeping, and winter cooking; the main family living space was outside in the yard. There was little furniture; storage baskets hung from the walls and the intricately carved ceiling beams. The yards often contained grapevines and convenient plots of vegetables, flowers, and herbs. Though the houses were arranged on streets, they were not built in direct line with their neighbors. The closeness of the houses and the amount of time people spent outside under the arbors meant that most activities could be seen and heard by the neighbors. Everyone knew everyone else's business.

The Cherokee idea of communal life was also built into the physical arrangement of the village. Communal structures in the center of town included a storage area for grain and a Town House or Council House large enough to accomodate most of the adult population. Outside the palisade, there was a spacious outdoor area for dancing and playing sports. People willingly gave time and effort to build and maintain these community projects.

In the Cherokee villages, there were no starving poor and no people of enormous wealth. Most worked extremely hard. The staples were turkey and fish raised in the village, eaten with cornbread, cornmeal mush, grits, hominy, cornmeal pancakes, and dozens of kinds of beans. The villagers supplemented their diet by hunting birds, squirrels, possums, raccoons, and deer. They gathered greens, bird eggs, wild berries, wild onions, mushrooms, nuts, grapes, and plums. Wild honey was prized. Maple sugar acquired through trading was a favorite sweetener. Hot pepper was applied liberally. Villagers made jerky and a variety of snacks resembling Cracker Jacks, trail mix, and granola bars.

Women had status equal to that of men. They took part in government and were trained to use weapons; in fact, it was the grandmothers alone who had the power to end war. The chiefs lived in typical village homes. The office of chief was viewed as a sacrifice of time and effort, and not as an arena for competition among prominent villagers. A good chief was highly respected, but little more than the person who did his work well in tending the turkey pen.

Life was not always easy. There was a constant fear of war and of raids; a team of watchmen remained prepared in case of attack. There was almost no crime within the villages, however. Rape and child molesting were very rare, and domestic violence was stopped by community intervention and censure at its onset. Striking a child under any circumstances was considered abusive. Most homes had neither locks nor solid doors, yet there was little vandalism or juvenile delinquency. Antisocial activities were considered signs of mental illness; about one adult in five had some form of training in counseling, and there were no charges, no waiting, and no stigma involved in arranging an appointment. If, in the end, a villager insisted upon stealing, hating his mother, or attacking people, it would probably be decided that he had given himself over to evil spiritual forces, and he would be made to leave the community.

Villagers were expected to shoulder their responsibilities and to work hard, yet some of the characters in these stories don't work hard and don't do what the community expects. In some stories, bravery and the ability to fight are held up as great virtues, while in others it is clear that peace is longed for. In some stories, family closeness is celebrated, while in others the rights of the individual are of greater importance. It would be wrong, though, to assume that Cherokee people were ambivalent when these values seemed to come in conflict, or that situational ethics prevailed. The Cherokee ethic is based on the assumption that human morals are frail, that emotions can be overpowering, and that intelligence and perception are highly fallible. People should be corrected with tolerance, love, and humor; to become infuriated at minor transgressions or to harbor grudges is to cultivate a further fault. It is far better to be humble and to strive toward the central tenet of Cherokee belief—balance or harmony, the Orinda.

The Cherokee villages deep in the forest are gone. Most of the forest has disappeared as well. But Cherokee people past and present have kept alive their views of reality and the stories in which their ideas are embodied. The old ways had something of value, something which should not be lost or forgotten, something which may help us deal better with the world we live in here and now.

TALES FROM THE CHEROKEE HILLS

ᒍᐱᏟᎾ
It Begins

Darkness and cold, deep and endless;
Wind blowing across bare rock unceasingly;
High up on the arch of stone
The small ones curled in sleep began to know
That the rock was cold and hard,
Wind never stopped,
There was no room,
And, even in sleep, they felt the void,
Unthinkable space stretching overhead,
And, on all sides,
A fearful drop.
Someone among the sleepers woke:
And, moaning, suffering, one by one,
They woke to thirst and fear and darkness,
Their cries carried away on the wind.
A hesitant voice whispered, "Water—
I smell it far below.
And I am Water Beetle! Water Beetle I am!"
He tottered to the edge and jumped.
Far below, they heard a splash.
Someone said, "I can—I can make a thread.
And I am Spider, that is who I am!"
And, one by one, the beings came to life,
Stirred, uncurled, staggered upright.
Water Beetle called up to them,
"Under the water, there is something,
Soft, not hard, with room for all."
Someone called out,
"Lift it up—make ropes, raise it above the water."
And ropes were made,
Creatures sliding down them,
Diving in the water, fastening the slab of mud,

And all of them hauling, pulling,
Until it rose above the waters,
And then all the beings
Scrambled down in the darkness,
Down the ropes, over and under each other,
Down the ropes, down to the mud,
To the water's edge,
And, when their thirst was satisfied,
Some, finding they were fishes, swam away,
Others, discovering wings, knew they were birds.
Turtles and frogs sank happily in the mud,
While the rest lay exhausted, no longer thirsting,
No longer crouched on the rock
In fear of the void.
And there it stays, our world,
Hung by the ropes from the stone arch of the sky,
Above the deep waters,
Until the day, destined to come,
When the ropes fray apart,
And it sinks once again beneath the waters.

ᏍᎳᎥᏯᏁ ᏣᏍᎷᏁᏍᎳᏥᏀ~ᏂᎥ

Coming of the Light

High on the stone arch
I wakened to the cold, the dark, and fear,
And others around me, moaning and shivering.
The brush of fur,
Of feathers, scales, and hardened shell
Against my skin
Made me know
That I was naked to the wind.
I cried out.
Someone answered, and I knew
I am one who cries and who is answered.
There were voices and jostling and movement,
And, almost before I knew,
I was shoved over the edge,
Scrambling down a rope,
Overrun by faster climbers.
Landing, far below, in the mud,
I drank my thirst away,
And, crouched in the mud beside the waters,
I called again,
And heard the sounds of someone,
Pushing, shoving, crawling toward me,
And another, more.
Muddy fingers, trembling, touched my face
As I touched all their faces, weeping.
We formed a circle, arms around each other,
And were warm.
I learned to smile, to laugh then. This is who I am.
Around us, fish found the water, birds their wings,
One especially, a giant of his kind,
Flying low, fanning the mud,
Struck it and scraped it,

Piling it higher and higher.
And some of us crept to the heights.
Something calling to us
To live on high ground.
Yet we were still unsatisfied,
Cold, fearful of the dark,
Though not knowing anything else;
Still, as we knelt together on the height,
Thinking of an opposite to darkness,
Strange powers came forth among us
As we longed for an end to the dark.
It was amazing:
A ball of light burst forth.
How did this come to be? We did not know.
Perhaps our need made us strong.
Perhaps it was not we who made it.
It appeared, that is all we knew,
And light was everywhere,
Light and heat. The creatures began to cry in pain:
It burned, it burned.
There was no escape, no rest in sleep;
It burned through closed eyelids.
And we, on the height in our circle,
Willed it higher, desperately.
Higher it went; our wills—
Or something answering our pleas—
Throwing it higher, and again higher, seven times,
And made it move,
Across the stone arch of the sky,
And down, bringing the darkness once again.
We waited, for a voice on the wind told us
Light would return.
Long it seemed we endured, until that dawn,
Light slowly spreading across the sky,

The beautiful mountains rising, row on row,
Waters washing silver on the shore,
Bird-people floating in the air, fish in the waters,
And, one by one,
Each being finding out who he was,
His name and powers.

ᏍᎳ ᎠᏍ ᎫᎾᏘ

Selu and Kanati

Up on Pilot Knob they lived, all alone,
Selu and Kanati with their son,
The two of them never feeling their loneliness.
All the long years together, she was all he wanted,
And she, too, needed only Kanati her husband
To be neighbor, friend, family, and lover.
In her house, so carefully tended,
She fixed good food to feed them,
And he, whose name meant Lucky Hunter,
Always brought back game.
But though the house was warm with love,
The child felt lonely.
Was it, perhaps,
That the parents were so happy in their love
They failed to know this?
He played by the river every day,
Not far away—they thought it was safe enough.
And, from the bushes by the water's edge,
They could hear laughter.
Funny, it sounded like two children,
Laughing there.
"Oh well," they thought, "he's having fun. Why not?"
"I had fun with my friend today,"
The little boy said.
"He's coming again tomorrow."
"Well, that'll be good," said his father.
"Where's he come from?"
"Out of the water," said the boy.
"Well, who is he?" said his mother, teasing.
"Who's his family?"
"He's my older brother, he says.
And he got thrown away in the water."

Could this be? It was a strange time,
The world not so old as it is now,
And besides, Kanati and Selu
Knew of stranger things themselves.
"When he comes tomorrow, call me
And hold him tight," Kanati said.
When his playmate came,
He was challenged to a wrestling match,
And as soon as Kanati's son held the boy fast,
He called for help.
"No," cried the Wild Boy. "No,
You threw me away, you threw me away,"
For he was formed from the blood
Selu washed from the game she cleaned.
They carried Wild Boy to the house.
A child needs a family, after all,
And their son needed his friend.
But when they thought they were taming him,
Holding him there
And feeding him good food, kind words,
And the touch of soft hands,
They had only made him sly,
Obedient when in sight.
What were they to him? Something that stood
Between him and freedom,
Creatures who could force him into a box
(And that was all he saw in their neat house),
Givers of tidbits he could cajole from them.
And the child, Younger Brother?
Was he running partner, pet,
Toy for a morning's amusement?
Selu, a loving mother,
Saw a child who needed love,
Her son, knowing only kindness,

Saw no evil in Wild Boy,
And, calling him Elder Brother,
Followed where he led.
Only the father, Kanati the hunter,
Man of the forests,
Sometimes looked into those wild eyes
And wondered
Who or what he had let into his house.

ᏔᎵ ᎣᏪᏥᏓ

Wild Boy

What can parents do in a case like this?
Selu and Kanati were helpless.
They'd never had any trouble before they took in
Wild Boy to raise.
But now, all of a sudden,
They had *two* wild boys, not one.
Elder Brother led Younger Brother into mischief.
Sometimes it was harmless,
Just fun that went too far,
But sometimes
It was as if Wild Boy were really that—
A wild animal in boy's skin.
Wild Boy thought about things
Younger Brother never thought of—
"Why is it Father never comes home
Without game to eat?" he asked.
"Where does he go?"
They followed him.
Kanati never thought of it.
Younger Brother, before Wild Boy came,
Stayed close to home and asked few questions.
Kanati came to a place on the side of a hill,
A cave, whose mouth was covered by a rock.
He heaved the rock aside, and out sprang a deer;
He shot it neatly, shouldered it, and went home.
"I want to see what's in there," said Wild Boy.
Together, their strength was enough
To move the rock.
But the first deer springing from the cave
Bowled them both over,
Tumbling them down the hillside.
What happened next was so astonishing

The boys didn't even try to replace the rock.
Hundreds of deer, raccoons, rabbits ran out,
Pouring down the hill, jumping over their heads,
Running around them;
Game birds of all kinds flew out.
The noise they made was almost deafening.
In fact, Kanati, sitting at home, heard the sound,
And, getting to his feet, he told his wife,
"Our bad boys have gotten into trouble.
I'd better take a look."
As he walked through the woods full of deer,
Raccoons, and squirrels, he knew.
The boys were still standing there astonished,
By the mouth of the cave,
Too astounded to move.
Without a word, Kanati went into the cave
And released from a jar
The wasps, mosquitoes, flies,
And all the other bugs that plague us now,
Who promptly surrounded the two boys
In a cloud of misery.
"Well," he said,
"That's not the last misery you'll feel.
You've had life easy, boys,
When all you had to do was wait for your meat.
From now on, you'll have to work for it,
And I guess I will, too.
I'll try to get us something for supper tonight,
And you go on home and see if your mother
Can soothe your bites and stings."
Life was hard indeed, they decided.
By the time they got home,
They were itchy, tired, discouraged, and hungry.
"We have no meat left," Selu said,

"But sit in the shade,
Put this lotion on your itchy places,
And I'll find you something."
And off she went,
To the storage shed behind the house.
"Let's follow her," said Wild Boy.
"The storage place is empty.
If she gets us something to eat,
I want to know how she does it."
And, with Younger Brother,
He peeked into the shed through cracks.
Once again, they saw a strange sight.
Selu was dancing and prancing,
And rubbing her stomach
As she leaned over her basket,
And the basket was filling up with corn and beans!
They dashed back to their places
Under the shade arbor;
When Selu came out
With bowls of corn and beans for them,
Their innocent faces
Should have told her something,
But when they wouldn't touch their food,
She knew what had happened.
"I must leave you now," she said,
"Before the sun goes down.
I wanted to stay with you and raise you
Until you were grown,
Until you were done with mischief,
But now you'll have to grow up without a mother,
And that's the way it is."
"Where are you going?" said Younger Brother,
His eyes full of tears.
"Away to the Nightland, my darling child,
To the Land of Death."

And Wild Boy never said a word.
"Before I die, you must hurry, hurry, children.
Clear the land and dig up the ground,
All around the house.
Dig as much as you can, before the sunset,
And, when I die,
Drag my body around the house seven times,
Plant me in the ground,
Sprinkle water all around the ground,
Wait and watch all night, and, in the morning,
You will have plenty,
For food will grow from the ground.
Oh, think of me, remember me,
Know that my love is with you
When you eat the corn from the ground."
She grew weaker, weaker, kissed them both,
And died with the setting sun.
They did as she said.
In the dawn light,
Kanati came home, asking the boys in surprise,
"Where is your mother?"
Stammering, weeping, Younger Brother told him,
Pointing to the cornfield,
"She's still with us, Father."
Kanati would not go into the house again
Now that it was cold and empty.
"I am leaving," he told the boys.
Kanati went travelling alone, wandering.
Ever alone, in sorrow,
He went through all the land,
And, passing to the Darkened Land,
He wandered still,
Finally passing beyond it
To the place where the sun goes down.
There, waiting for him, he found his wife,
And there, together, they live
Needing nothing more, needing nothing more.

ᎣᏃᏫ ᎠᎴᎥᏏ ᎢᏳᏓ

Firebringer

Grandmother's little black eyes gleamed
And that was all the sign she showed
Of what she thought
As she stood, hands calmly folded,
And listened, as we all did,
To the plans of the leaders,
The strong ones, the brave, the famous,
To gain the prize
From the island.
Her thin, frail-seeming body bent more and more
And her long, thin nose seemed almost to twitch
As each one contended to be first.
"I'm strongest," shouted Bear, the Red Chief.
"But strength alone won't win.
I'm fast," said Eagle proudly.
"Ah, yes," said Buzzard, "but I can outwit you all."
"Granny," whispered the youngest child,
"You could do it better than any of them."
But she said not a word:
She only smiled,
And we knew that we'd get more out of this
Than warm houses and hot dinners,
Though that was plenty. We were all tired
Of cold cereal and raw vegetables
For breakfast, lunch, and dinner.
Well, back they all straggled,
Scorched, singed, and defeated.
As they sat there dejected on the lakeshore,
Grandmother straightened her back,
Clapped her hands together,
And spoke for the first time.
"Little ones, get me clay," she said.
"Get me moss, wet moss."
And she rolled and coiled the clay in her hands.

"Oh, run and get me
My smallest berry basket," she called.
As everybody slowly turned and watched,
She lined the basket with the coils of clay,
Lined the clay with the moss,
And, stepping lightly,
Grandmother Spider
Crossed the lake to the island.
She gathered hot coals
From the burning tree stump into the basket
And returned.
"Quick, get pine knots, children.
Bring sticks, make torches, young folks.
Each mother take a fire for her home.
Men, quick, make hearths from stones."
And when our hearth was lighted,
And the smoke rose to the Above Ones
In a visible prayer of thanks,
She tipped out the burned moss and dead coals,
Pulled off the woven withes,
And, stepping to the stream,
Showed us her second present,
A hard basket made of clay that could hold water!
Grandmother's little black eyes
Gleamed in our firelight,
And she smiled her small, modest smile.

ᏙᏓᏍᎠ ᏴᏏᏒᎢ

Thunder

Each spring, people planted Selu's gift;
Gardens grew larger
As they watched what the animals ate,
And learned new plants to grow.
Voices spoke on the wind
To ears that heard,
Visions came
To those who looked for them.
Strange and fearful tales were told on winter nights
And some of them were so.
Travellers whispered of a giant snake
With poison blood
In a land far to the north.
One misty evening late in the fall
A hunter gathering firewood
Heard the crash of breaking brush
On a ridge above him.
Following the sound of fighting,
As the mists thinned out, he saw
An enormous, thrashing snake,
Covered with glistening scales,
And, almost buried in the coils, a man.
"Help me, Nephew, help me," gasped the man,
"He's your enemy as well as mine!"
And the hunter shot, powerful and true,
Through the monster's body.
The coils snapped loose,
And, in its dying convulsions,
The snake fell
Crashing down the hillside to the valley below.
Its victim stood,
And the hunter saw he was no mortal,

But the Red Man of the Lightning.
He was Thunder, glowing as he stood.
From the body of the snake, he took a scale,
Making it into a charm for finding game,
And he told that hunter many secret things,
So that the snakes of the north
And the monsters of the night
No longer needed to be feared
By the friends of Thunder.
In this way, little by little,
Led by visions, befriended by Powers,
Listening to the voices on the wind,
The people gained knowledge
Of things of the spirit.

ᏊᎦᏖᎠ
Uk'ten'

Speak of snakes in low voices in broad daylight,
Of monster snakes in whispers, saying little,
And never in the dark.
They say that all of them were men once,
Changed by conjuration
To do some desperate thing,
Their bodies growing longer,
Arms and legs shrinking, disappearing,
Skin getting dry and scaly,
Heads growing small and flat,
Eyes little and hot, brain turning,
Turning, fury turned to poison
Dripping from their mouths.
Uk'ten', they say, was a fearsome creature,
His body so thick
Only a tall man could see over him,
Heavy with men he had eaten.
His scales glittered, his wicked horns gleamed,
And on his forehead was a blazing crystal,
Large as a man's two fists.
They say that gem dazed men, fascinated them,
So that, entranced,
They blindly ran toward the snake
And so were killed.
But once a man went hunting Uk'ten'.
Some say he was a conjuror, a man of magic,
One who would risk anything for power,
But some say
He was that hunter who helped Thunder
When the Red Man fought
Another of those snakes;
No matter, this man knew a secret:

How Uk'ten' may be killed.
Now everyone knew
Uk'ten' liked the dark, lurked in lonely places,
Dark passes in the mountains, bogs and marshes,
And under deep, dark pools in streams,
Waiting for men to come unwarily;
Waiting for men to eat.
The hunter went from likely place to likely place;
He tried deep spots in the rivers,
Under shaded banks,
And dived where the water was dark.
He moved cautiously through the highlands,
Through the dark trees.
Finally, at dawn, in a high pass,
He saw Uk'ten', asleep.
Backing away, without a sound, he crept off,
Ran down the mountain,
And gathered wood from seven trees,
Making seven fires.
Yes, all the way up the mountain,
Placing on each as he lighted it
A pinch of the seven kinds of dried leaves
For making sacred smoke.
Looking back down the slope
As he reached the summit
He could see the smoke
Begin to rise from seven fires,
And then it was he shot Uk'ten',
Through the seventh spot on its side,
Tearing through its heart,
And, turning toward his fires, began to run,
As, behind him,
The dying monster belched out poison in a cloud.
The hunter held his breath
And jumped the first fire,

Then the second, third—
The cloud of death surrounded him,
And from behind, a stream of boiling, acid blood
Rolled down the hill.
At the seventh fire,
Able to hold his breath no more,
He gasped, and breathed only smoke,
Smoke of the seven woods,
Smoke of the pipe.
He saw the stream of blood
Turn aside from the fire,
And stood behind it, safe at last.
The monster's uncoiled body went rolling down,
Crushing all in its path,
Scavengers following.
From the dead body
The hunter pried what he wanted:
The crystal, large as a man's two fists,
Transparent as water,
With a blood-red vein down the middle,
Stone of prophecy, stone of power,
Stone that must have blood
Before it speaks.

ᏪᏌ

Bear

That boy loved the woods.
When Yona was so little
His legs were too short to keep up,
The big boys learned to take him anyway.
He always knew
Where the fattest, ripest berries were,
Where the trout were hiding in the pools,
Where the nuts were thickest.
He began to go out all alone, whenever he could,
Finally, getting up before his parents
So they wouldn't tell him not to go,
Staying longer and longer.
His parents worried,
Especially when he missed dinner
And hadn't had breakfast. Why, that wasn't right!
But still, he was always bringing his mother
Combs of wild honey, baskets of nuts,
Fresh mushrooms, greens, berries—
Why, they could have lived
Off the trout he caught alone!
Finally they spoke to him.
"Yona, we never see you at home all day.
That shouldn't be; what's going on?"
His answer amazed them.
He simply held out his arms for them to see:
They were covered with long, brown fur.
"I can't stand sleeping
Under a roof anymore," he said.
"Eat at home?
I can eat better in the woods, and soon
I'll live there all the time."
His parents begged him to stay at home;

Clearly, something strange
Was happening to him in the woods.
"Oh, it's a better place, better than here,
And I'm changing, I'm changing.
I can't stay, no matter what you say or do.
Come with me, Mother, Father,
Come with me there—
There's plenty of food in the forest.
You know that; I've brought you some.
You'll never have to work again,
Never sweat in the sun hoeing corn,
Never haul water from the spring,
Never sleep behind hot and stuffy walls,
But sleep on soft moss, live with walls of trees
And a roof of stars."
Oh, to live free, to run in the wind,
To be strong, to have plenty!
So they told the people of the village,
And they all, every one,
Fasted and prayed for seven days,
And at dawn they left their houses,
Left them forever.
Messengers from other towns
Found them as they walked.
But they were changing, they were changing;
They could not stay.
"Come into the woods when you are hungry.
Find us. We shall come to give you our flesh."
They sang,
And they taught the messengers their song,
And then went on their way.
Looking back, the messengers saw only bears
Going up the mountain into the forest,
The words of the song drifting back on the wind:
"Surely we shall see each other,
Surely we shall see each other."

ᏗᏡᏗ

Spirit Defenders

Oh, once I was a good man in a fight,
A good hunter, too.
But now I leave that for my sons;
I am too old. Why, I have grandsons who are men,
Sitting in Council.
That's why they left me in the town last fall,
When all the men went hunting.
It was a time of peace, we thought,
And so they left no defenders. Only me,
A man with a broken leg, and a few small boys.
The women were out picking corn.
I heard a scream, and here the raiders came.
I threw my tomahawk
And ran for my bow,
Hoping only to shoot down one
Before they killed me.
But when I turned to shoot
(Oh, they were close—I don't run fast anymore)
I heard a bowstring twang behind me,
And at my right hand
I saw a stranger, shooting.
As I fired, and reached for another arrow,
I could see
A line of strangers, painted for battle.
Stranger still, as they fought, they sang.
In the fury of the fighting, calmness came to me,
A strange peace, strength
I never knew in my young years.
Forward we went against them.
By this time, the women of my town
(Brave as the men of other places)
Had gathered the children in the Council House,

Had gotten their bows and blowguns,
Now were firing from behind our line, a few
Creeping through the fields,
Cutting them down from behind.
Somewhere in the fight I found an ax;
We struggled hand to hand for seeming hours,
And then they broke.
Suddenly they were running, they were gone.
Niquasi once again was safe.
I turned to speak to the strangers,
To give them thanks,
Ask where they came from, in so timely a way.
They, too, were gone, instantly, without a trace.
Then I observed
They left no footprints on the ground;
Only the bodies of the enemy they had slain
Remained behind them.
I am singing when I greet the dawn
The song the spirit warriors taught to me.
I am singing, what few dawns remain to me in life,
Until with the spirits I will praise the dawn.

DWSA

Hidden Lake

He didn't know it would be like this.
When the old men showed their battle scars
And told their tales,
They said nothing
Of this weakness that overwhelmed him,
This obscenity of pain. He couldn't even tell
Where he hurt or how.
It hurt all through his body.
They didn't tell of that.
It was hard to move,
Harder to know which way to move.
The sky above him
Lightened and darkened in waves.
One fixed purpose
Grew and filled his mind: get under cover.
He was ashamed to die as a wounded animal,
Put out of its misery.
With an effort that seemed
As if he were trying to move the earth,
He rolled over, under some bushes,
And from there, into a gully.
Once started, mindlessly he kept moving,
Inches at a time.
In flashes, at lengthening intervals,
He wondered
Where he had dropped his bow, his knife.
They had trained him well.
He could wake up standing, knife in hand,
At a sudden sound. Now, weaponless,
He wondered if he was a warrior still,
When he thought at all.
More and more, he was only this:

Broken, hurting, alive, thirsty.
It was dark.
He proved to himself he was alive by moving,
By feeling pain.
He never knew
If that darkness was the world's night
Or only his darkening senses,
For that journey seemed to go on for days.
But at the end, like a deer, he could smell water,
And then his fingers touched it.
He lurched forward, into the soothing coolness.
When he awoke,
He was lying on his back in the shallows,
In the pearly light of dawn.
There was no pain, no fear.
He lay in safety and in peace.
He sat up.
Next to him lay a bear, asleep;
Beyond it, a deer, a fox.
The silver ripples washed the blood
From fur and feathers all along the shore.
It was the Hidden Lake,
The place that hunters cannot find,
The Medicine Lake
Where animals go to be healed.
When he returned to his home,
His voice was never raised
When the warriors told their tales
And showed their wounds.
In the dawn light,
He gave his thanks alone.

ᏨᏩᏖᎵᏓ

Tsuwatel'da

High up on Pilot Knob I heard the drumming,
The sound of rattles, sound of dancing feet,
And laughing voices, young girls' voices,
Calling in the woods. I searched.
I spent my childhood searching; as a young man
I was given a bad name.
"He's lazy," they all said. "Wanders the woods
Instead of working. Like as not
Brings back no meat from hunting all that time."
I lived with relatives, going from house to house.
Not cruelly treated, no, but still, they laughed
And how could I explain?
They sent me out one day,
Loaded my pouch with parched corn,
Laughed and said,
"Come back with something this time;
Stay out there
Until you do." Helplessly I smiled and shrugged.
On the ridge below Pilot Knob I met a stranger.
"Why not come with me?" he said.
"Tsuwatel'da is my home, and it is your place, too,
For you have kinfolk there."
Up on Pilot Knob he led me,
At a cave mouth he said, "We go in here."
Deeper and deeper we followed the cavern
Into the mountain,
Walking for what seemed like hours.
Suddenly we came to an opening,
Stepped out into the light.
A valley lay before us,
Wrapped in the arms of the mountains.
Oh, the soil was rich and dark, corn tall,

Crops abundant. People ran to greet us,
Calling me Cousin.
They brought me to their chief, who honored me
By seating me at his fire.
In all the days I stayed there,
More and more it seemed a place of wonder,
A place of peace and deep contentment,
Where there was no scornful laughter.
"I must go back," I said with deep reluctance.
The chief replied, "You will not be satisfied to stay.
When you want to come to us,
You know the way."
Back in the village,
They laughed when I told my tale.
"You used to be dumb and lazy.
Now you're a liar," they said.
It was strange, but I felt nothing
When once I would have felt shame. But the town,
My friends, my relations,
I suddenly saw through new eyes.
I saw each fault, each meanness;
At my sister's house, the house my father built,
I was homesick for Tsuwatel'da.
I made up my mind that day, but first
I'd give them something new to talk about.
I took a witness with me up to Tsuwatel'da.
Then they believed me. "The girls—so fine!
The food! The dancing there!"
And they all cried, "Take us to Tsuwatel'da!"
"Fast for seven days. I'll see you then," I said.
They fasted and waited;
They'd seen their last of me.
Tsuwatel'da is my home, for I have kinsmen there.
High up on Pilot Knob
You can hear the drumming,

The sound of rattles, sound of dancing feet,
And in the woods, girls' voices calling
If you have kinsmen there,
And when you want to come,
You'll know the way to Tsuwatel'da.

ᏬᎳ
Yahula

Up on the mountain road
Where it dips in the hollow
Stand late at night in the dark
And listen for Yahula:
Perhaps he rides there still.
You'll hear the sound of bells
On the horses' halters,
The crack of the stock whip,
And the pounding hoofbeats,
Passing by, passing by, fading into the distance,
And, drifting back to you, calling you on,
Yahula's voice,
Singing songs you have never heard,
But want to hear again.
Yahula traded horses, travelling
Through all the Overhill towns,
The Underhill and beyond.
He was a man with a hundred friends—
They loved to hear his bells
Announce his coming.
He disappeared while hunting
With men from his village.
They looked for him for days.
Reluctantly, grieving, they went home
To tell his family. Weeks passed.
Imagine their surprise
One misty evening just at twilight
They saw him come in the door.
He sat down at his place—they had left it empty—
At the supper table,
As quietly as if he had simply been away trading.
His wife, rejoicing, started to get his favorite foods,

To call his friends, to celebrate together.
He told her
He would never taste human food again:
He'd been with the Nunnehi.
Yes, the Immortals
Had found him on the mountain,
Hopelessly lost, had rescued him, taken him home
To their town.
And in the beautiful place, the land of peace,
No one could understand Yahula's sadness,
His quiet longing
For those he loved.
But that homecoming was as sad as it was happy,
For he could come to them, but could not stay.
Again and again, this man who loved his family
Returned to them, coming quietly in at the door,
And sadly, each time, he left them.
No words or tears could hold him
From his return to the Immortals.
It was strange.
Yahula had loved his travels, his adventures,
His many friends, his life,
Riding the trails alone, seeing new sights,
Always cheerfully singing as he rode;
Now it was over, without regret,
As if it had never been,
And, in the end, it mattered less to him
Than a dream, soon forgotten.
No, it was the family he loved
That he returned to.
These loved ones long ago have gone.
The house they lived in,
Even the town, are there no longer.
Perhaps the travellers late at night

May hear the sound of bells,
And the singing voice of Yahula the trader
On his travels once again.

ᎠᏂᏴᏩ ᎩᏍᎩ

Hunters among Us

How do I know what's the truth of it?
When I was a little boy, they used to tell me
Just the same thing you were told, probably:
"Get up, it's almost daylight;
The Hunters are among you!"
I, too, had nightmares
Of water spirits with invisible arrows
Killing the people
That they found asleep after daybreak.
Everybody knows what fever dreams are like:
Your childhood terrors
All come back to you, like as not.
I was certainly sick enough for anything
That time in Tiqualitsi town.
The people I was staying with
Got me help, but I kept getting sicker.
The elders kept trying out new remedies,
Which did no good.
They all got scared as I got worse, and, in the end,
They left me alone in the house to die.
Well, I really thought
It was going to be the end of me,
And I felt so bad I almost didn't care.
As I lay there, too sick to get up,
I saw in the doorway a stranger, an old woman.
"Well, they've all left you now," she said.
"I'll tell you what, if you come with me,
I'll make you well."
She was so matter-of-fact about it
I almost laughed.
Get out of bed and go with her? I wished I could.
But then she said again, "Come with me,"

And suddenly I felt stronger,
Or maybe more desperate, I don't know.
And I staggered up.
She got me to my feet and out the door.
We walked to the water; calmly she waded in.
I followed; the water rose around us,
Higher and higher.
She stooped under the surface; I followed,
Ducking my head
As if to pass under a low doorway,
Just as she had done.
Before us was a trail. We walked it.
We came to a village, just a village, like any other,
Full of people going about their business,
Ordinary, I thought,
Until I saw the Hunters coming,
And from the poles on their shoulders
Hung the dead bodies of people.
Yes, people I knew, some of them.
I walked on, I walked on, as if in a dream;
She led me to her house.
She wrapped me in warm blankets by her fire
And said, "You must be hungry."
The smell of frying meat filled the house;
When she brought me a dish of it,
I remembered those Hunters
And turned my head away.
"Oh," she said, "I see you cannot eat our food."
And she fixed me corn and beans.
Days went by, weeks went by; I was stronger.
At last, she told me I was well; I must go home,
But not to speak for seven days.
This I obeyed,
Making signs at my throat to the people
As if I could not talk.

They were surprised to see me;
They thought I'd died,
Thought I'd wandered away in the woods
In my fever after they'd left.
They took care, I noticed,
To stay away until I could speak,
For fear of catching something.
Well, one thing I learned:
I'm better off with *no* friends
Than the ones I thought I had at Tiqualitsi town.
But about the rest of it
I don't know what to think.
If there really are Hunters among us,
One of them sure did me a good turn
When so-called friends would have let me die.
But why? She never said.
And all of it was like a dream.
In broad daylight,
I think, like any sensible man, I dreamed.
But yet at dusk I shiver to see dark water
And ripples on the stream.

AWO DB₽OĐY
The Raven Mockers

Whisper the words.
Say that name as little as you can,
Don't draw their attention.
Raven Mockers.
They can look old or young, man or woman,
Beautiful, ugly, kind, mean.
Have you seen a shower of fiery sparks
Streaking across the night sky,
Heard a rushing sound like a windstorm
When no leaf stirs?
You've heard their passing then,
On their way to a new deathbed.
Shiver when you hear a raven's cry
Where no bird is.
It means another being gone to the Land of Death
A few hours, a few days early,
What was left of his life
Stolen by a Raven Mocker
To add those hours to his own life.
They add an hour, a day, every time they can;
And they have been watching us
For long, long years,
Their prey—the sick and injured.
All the kin can stand around the bed watching,
All in vain.
The Mockers take the shape of others,
Seeming to be old Grandfather, Grandson,
Wife, harmless friend,
Sweetly speaking, coming closer,
Placing a gentle hand on the forehead,
Looking at the helpless one
With pitiless two-hundred-year-old eyes,

Waiting, waiting, until heads turn,
Until others leave the room,
Then, in a flash, ripping out the heart,
They creep off to their hiding place
And eat the life, the heart, in secret.
Once a man out hunting
Was caught by nightfall far from home.
He saw a house deep in the trees, and,
Finding no one home, lay down to wait,
Curled up in a corner.
He fell asleep in the dark there,
Waking in cold terror to the cry of a giant raven.
An old man came in the door,
Grumbling to himself,
"She's late, always late.
Probably expects *me* to cook the supper."
The hunter, ready to laugh at his silly fears,
Started to speak,
But then there came the call of another raven,
Coming closer.
"Oh, there you come at last,"
The old man muttered.
An old woman hobbled in, smiling sweetly.
"What luck did you have?" her husband asked.
"Nothing. They watched the whole time,
And would you believe it,
Had one of those magic charms,
One that worked, for once,
To keep off Raven Mockers!" And her low laugh
Chilled the unknown watcher.
"What about you?" she asked, and the old man,
Beaming a kindly smile, said,
"I always get what I'm after, my dear."
The watcher saw her take the meat, spit it,
And place it over the fire.

Suddenly she stood very still,
And slowly turned her head
From side to side. "I *smell* something," she said,
"Old fool, don't you?" And quicker than thought,
She thrust a torch into the fire
And ran about the room,
Poking it into all the dark corners.
The young man sat up in the torchlight,
Rubbing his eyes,
Pretending he had just awakened,
Explaining his presence
In slow, stammering words.
He giggled stupidly, claimed to be lost, and smiled
Until his face felt stiff,
Even offering to help Old Granny
To turn the spit,
Letting them know
He thought that was a piece of venison,
And not a human heart, still warm.
Well, next morning, they let him go.
Back he went to his village, as fast as he could run.
The wise ones knew what to do,
For Raven Mockers can be killed for seven days
Once they have taken their own guise to feed
And someone has seen them as they are:
They sleep in deathlike slumber.
They found the evil ones entranced,
And cleansed the world
Of them and their possessions
With fire.
Standing all around the house
As the burning rafters fell,
As the smoke rose,
As the fire sank down to cinders and ash,
They stood, shivering with cold,

For they knew, as we all know,
That these who love life so much
That they would steal it
Are not evil strangers, but kinsmen,
And every Raven Mocker
Is one of us,
One of us.

DhPᏃᏂ
Spirit Panthers

The other women tell me to stop crying.
They say, "You have a husband, other children—
Think of them."
Oh, they should tell the wind
When it should blow,
Tell clouds not to rain.
I've lost Tuya twice; how many tears
Is the proper number for that?
Tuya, my son, what is he doing,
Right now, this moment?
Does he dream at night of us?
(I hope he never mourns as I do now.)
He went out to gather kindling. It was late in fall.
The weather changed in hours; it began to snow,
The earliest we had known it.
Tuya didn't come home.
I called, I called,
I walked out to the edge of the fields.
It got dark.
His father searched,
Came home wet and exhausted,
Searched again. In the night,
The wind grew stronger, colder.
Ponds were frozen the next morning.
"If he's out in that, he did not survive,"
The wise ones said
Still we tried, my husband, my brothers,
All in vain.
As the snow melted, many days later,
Here came Tuya,
Muddy, but well and strong.
How we hugged him, how we cried then
With tears of joy.

The story he told was strange:
He'd gotten lost in the blizzard, turned around,
Unable to find the way,
Falling down in the snow exhausted
At the end; he awakened
When something gripped his neck,
Dragging him out of the snow, into a cave.
This being, and others with it, wrapped him warm
And put him close to their fire. They were, he said,
Panthers, as large as people.
Yes, that was the tale that Tuya told us,
Panthers with a fire!
They told him that he should not eat their food,
But after days, the storm did not abate;
They feared for him
And so they finally fed him.
Oh, there are other beings,
Tuya says, beyond the cave,
That look like us, like people,
And they spoke with him,
When the storm ended,
Before they sent him home.
Oh, to have Tuya home and safe!
I fixed his favorite food.
But when he began to eat,
Tuya turned pale and wretched.
Nothing I fixed him would stay down.
I held him while his stomach heaved.
I fixed him medicine; nothing helped.
"No, Mother," Tuya said, "I was told
Once I had eaten in the underworld,
I could not eat our food. I must return."
I dressed him in his best,
I packed his toys, his bow.
I let him go and followed him to the cave,

But when I got there,
The opening turned to blank stone,
No way in for me.
And who is caring for my son now?
Will he grow as other children do?
And will I have grandchildren in that place
That they have barred me from with stone?
Oh, Tuya, I think of you, I think of you.

DILA
Shapechanger

He'd been a marked man for three years,
A Bowshooter,
His hair worn loose and waistlength
With a small, single braid in front of his left ear,
Telling the world he was dangerous,
A fighter to the death.
He had yet to be afraid in battle, this young man,
For in the end everyone dies.
But in the dawn of that morning
When he heard the enemy had tricked them,
Was ahead of them,
Would surely reach the village before them,
He knew, with sudden cold conviction,
Warning from the watchmen wasn't enough,
And he became afraid then.
His Raven Leader, understanding, let him go.
He ran, well ahead of the others,
He reached the stream.
He saw the tracks in wet clay from their crossing:
Hours old; he was too late.
Alone, he knelt there, trying to calm himself,
Trying to empty his mind of fear, of anger,
Trying to find his balance,
His harmony with all life.
Holding a mussel shell
Lightly in his cupped hands,
He asked, and the Helpers replied.
(Ah, desperate men do desperate deeds.)
He climbed into the canoe
That magic made from the shell,
He paddled upstream until, shaky from the effort,
He saw the village on the bank, deserted,

All but one house.
There, in front of her doorway,
Sat his grandmother,
Calmly waiting for the raiders,
For the coming death.
He knelt before her, silently pleading.
"No," she said, turning her head away,
"It is my home, built by the hands of my husband,
My bridal house, the place my babies were born.
No, I will not come away."
"Sticks and mud," he said.
"Only sticks and mud that you would die for.
Home to me," he said, "is where you are.
Very well, if you stay to die with your home,
I will stay to die with mine,"
And, sitting on the ground beside her,
He threw away his weapons of war.
It was then she cried
And threw her arms around him,
Child of her dead child, only grandson, only kin.
"Too late," she wept,
As they heard
The pounding footsteps of the raiders.
"No," he said, and laughing in triumph,
Made her small, tucked her into the gourd canteen
At his belt,
And, transformed into a bird,
Rose into the sky.

ᎠᏂᏍᎦᏫ ᏗᎰᏗᏍ
Incubus

He wasn't a baby. He was a big boy,
Big enough this fall to go with the others
To gather nuts, to carry water for Mother,
To bring in kindling wood.
That was the trouble, he thought.
Father said he was old enough to hunt—
He was even helping him
Make a boy-sized bow—
But when he wanted to play by the forest cliff, "No.
Too young," Father said.
Father didn't understand.
The cliff was his own place, his and Brother's.
They could make play-forts, and secret paths
Deep in the blackberry thickets
No grown-up could enter,
And they had found their best place,
Their secret cave
Only last week,
Just a scooped-out place under a ledge,
But theirs, and secret, a place to put treasures.
Today Mother was busy,
Stringing peppers and beans to dry,
And Father was gone to the Council House,
So he decided to go back one last time.
No use to ask Brother—he wouldn't do it
If Father said no.
It was different this time,
Secret, but there was no pleasure in it.
Today it seemed farther, and, for the first time,
He was aware that if he called for help,
No one from his village could hear.

The air seemed hot and heavy;
The birds were silent;
The leaves hung still in the heat.
There was someone in the cave,
Someone not quite human,
Small, but seeming grown-up, somehow.
The boy was afraid, yet not willing to admit it,
Since the Little Man was half his size.
The creature smiled winningly.
The boy was charmed.
"Carry me on your back," it said,
"Give me a little ride."
The boy obeyed.
At first, it was a good game.
He danced and cavorted, pranced in circles.
Soon, though, his burden grew heavy.
The boy tired.
"Get down," he said.
The only answer was a laugh, wild and inhuman,
That echoed from the cliffs.
Soon the boy felt an odd sensation:
The skin of his back was sticking to the creature.
It was growing into his flesh.
"Help me," he prayed,
And far down the mountainside,
The song of Brown Whippoorwill answered him;
He knew then what to do.
Climbing a tree, he pretended to slip, to fall.
When he lay motionless, trying not to breathe,
The creature left him,
Sighing, "How easily they die!
Such a good ride he was.
Now I'll just have to find another."

For weeks after that,
The boy was so good
His parents worried about him.
Oh, he also started to call himself Possum:
Nobody could figure out why.

ᎣᏳᎠ
Immortal

She was not the most beautiful girl among them,
Not even better looking then some in the village,
Yet once I looked at her,
She was the flower of them all:
She was herself, just that.
It was enough.
She was not one of those bold girls
Who flirt with all men.
Quiet, seemingly shy, eyes downcast,
She came into the dance arbor
Unknown to me,
Yet, before I heard her speak,
I was her man.
I spoke to her and those girls with her,
Welcoming her to my town,
To the Green Corn Dance.
Later, I walked with her to get water,
Held the gourd for her,
And her hand lightly touched mine.
It was hard to hold my hand steady
For her to drink.
I held her hand when we danced the Circle Dance,
And after
I sat at her feet,
Not touching,
But I knew to a hairsbreadth
How far away she sat.
After the dance, when they rose to leave,
I asked them if they had far to go,
Were the men of their town to meet them,
For they were six girls alone.
I called my friends; we walked with them

Down to the log bridge crossing the stream.
There, on the other side, they said,
Was their escort. On the way,
In the darkness, we held hands,
Exchanging whispers.
What did we say? Too little.
—Her name. She liked the dance. The night was
    beautiful.
—"Smell the honeysuckle." "We will meet again."
    "We will."
At the last, she said, "I will not forget."
They started across the footbridge,
And were no more.
They vanished into air.
The wise ones say they were Immortals,
Spirit Beings, who come
For reasons of their own among us.
Whatever the reason,
There is no woman that I'll marry
Since I have seen her,
Since I have heard her low, sweet whisper,
"We will meet again."

TOR RA
The Girl in the Tree

He was coming down the trail from the ridge at dusk;
As he reached the trees, he slowed his step.
Suddenly it was strange, as if he had never seen it;
The wind stopped, and in the silence
He heard a voice, faint and far.
Slowly, almost reluctantly, he turned toward it.
He, who had never been afraid in battle, hesitated,
Then went slowly forward into the dark wood,
Unwilling to make a sound. The call was louder,
A girl's voice, young, sweet, clear.
"Can you hear me? Oh, come help me
If you can.
I've waited and I've waited.
Are you coming? Oh, answer, answer!"
She broke into sobs, pathetic to hear.
And he saw her. A pale face, high in the tree,
Her beautiful hair, long and wild, streaming loose.
"Look up, Hummingbird.
Here I am, can you see me?
Oh, climb, climb up quickly,
Get me free."
He tried, fell back,
Jumped for the lowest branch,
Pulled up, reached again, looked up,
She was just as far above him
As when he stood on the ground.
He slipped, started over, climbed again;
Breathless, panting, he struggled,
Jumping higher for new handholds.
Still, high above him, he could see her wide eyes,
Her tear-marked cheeks. He slipped again.
As he paused, a hot tear fell on his hand.
"Oh, Hummingbird, don't stop now.

You'd almost reached me," she said.
He slid back down to the ground,
Staggered back from the tree,
And shook his head to clear it.
(How did she know me by name?
How did her voice reach me on the trail?
Why can't I reach her when I climb?)
Slowly, he turned away, slowly,
As if moving underwater,
He took one step, then another.
She cried, she whispered, she moaned.
He kept on walking.
At the edge of the clearing, he turned.
His eyes swept up the trunk of the tree,
And saw nothing,
Nothing more than bark, branches, leaves,
Bark, branches, leaves.
"Hummingbird, Hummingbird, find me.
Hummingbird, Hummingbird, set me free.
Don't you want to find me?
Don't you want to know
Who I am,
Why I need you,
What I can give you in return?"

4M
Selu

They say that anxious hunters kill no game.
That day, I had no chance to shoot and miss—
I would have rejoiced to see even a squirrel.
The smell of dust, of dry leaves,
I brought with me from my dying fields
Into the dying forest.
We'd hauled water in that drought
Ever-increasing distances
From drying creeks and springs
Until I thought my back would break, for little use.
Thought of my hungry ones drove me far-ranging
Over the mountain;
As it got dark, I heated thin cornmeal gruel
Over my fire.
Tired and discouraged, I slept and dreamed.
The sound of singing filled the little clearing,
Singing of unearthly beauty.
Next morning, I arose, ate my meager ration,
And set out,
And once again found nothing.
Once more, that night, I dreamed.
Now some may say it was my weariness,
Or lack of food.
I only say I saw my dreams broad waking,
And who am I to say what things are real?
Some old ones say this world we know is shadows,
That only dreams are real.
I only know that when I woke,
The singing of my dreams went on,
And I in wonder followed where it led,
Weariness, despair, and hunger
In that song forgotten.

The singing led me to a single corn plant,
Growing all alone in a glade,
Glowing like green fire against the dark trees.
The leaves whispered, and they spoke to me
As I knelt down before it,
Telling me to cut a single root,
And from it I would be fed,
To take others to feed my children.
It whispered, whispered;
It commanded
Always to share with others the bounty I would find.
The sun reached noon. The plant shimmered;
Suddenly, in a flash, the corn was gone,
Transformed
Into a woman, beautiful to see. She smiled,
And rose into the air, disappearing,
Leaving me alone.
Selu, Corn Mother,
It was she who spoke to me.
Was it a dream
That I arose from sleep and saw these things
Or was it real?
I only know that in my sleep sometimes
I catch the faint echo of that music
And I awake
In tears.

Dh

Strawberries

Oh, I think I married her too young, this girl.
Not yet ready to be serious and sober,
Head of the family,
Mother.
I come home, to find dinner not cooked,
Corn and squash not even picked to make dinner,
When everyone knows the best time is early,
Before the dew dries.
Here it is sunset, and where is she?
Out picking flowers.
I was angry,
But I was sad, too.
I had seen her beauty, and I married her too young.
In my guilt, I spoke impatiently.
It was not well done.

Oh, he doesn't understand.
He thinks I feel nothing for him,
Because I neglected dinner
And picked flowers instead.
I thought of him
When I followed the flowers into the forest,
Thinking of the day I saw his eyes gleam
When he looked at me,
And I knew that day he was thinking of me in his house
Cooking his meal.
Now he shows me he is sorry he thought of me.
Oh, he must show me that he loves me.
I will make him show me.

Next morning I awakened
And she was gone.
Outside I saw her footprints in the dew.
I followed, running.
Finally I saw her, too far ahead to catch,
And I longed for her to stop
So that I could speak to her tenderly,
And as I stood there, regretting it was too late,
Magic happened.
Wild strawberries grew at her feet.
She slowed, she stopped to pick them.
When I came up to her
Her mouth was sweet with them.

At first, I was not leaving him, not really.
I was teasing, playing.
I wanted to see him follow, show his love.
But when he ran behind, fear came over me
Without a reason, and I ran hard.
I could not stop.
Pride would not let me stop tamely for him.
When I saw the berries, it was magic.
I stopped, and when he came,
I told him the spirits had done this,
And I told him I was glad.

ᏣᎳᏫ ᎠᏎ ᎤᏝᏲᎯ

Hummingbird and Crane

Beauty she certainly had. To see her shining hair
Swing in the dance,
To see her move like a flower swaying
Made a man catch his breath.
Hard to blame her because she enjoyed her power,
Her chance to choose;
She would pretend to frown in displeasure,
Then award a smile. Of course she was spoiled.
One by one, her suitors found simpler girls
Who spent their days learning to cook,
To sew, to grow tall corn,
To be kind when they met kindness.
Her mother, her father said "Choose"
When the suitors dwindled to two.
Still she didn't know.
Hummingbird was quick and graceful.
He, too, made people catch their breath;
He was so beautiful she was almost jealous,
And, of course, nearly as pleased with himself as she.
Crane looked awkward beside him,
His powerful body bulky
Compared to the graceful dancer.
She set a test for them, a distance race,
Her marriage the prize.
(Because Crane was modest, she had never heard
That of all the warriors,
He endured the longest on the marches.)
At the signal, Hummingbird was off in a flash.
Crane lumbered behind, so slow
His rival's dust settled before he came.
But when it got dark, Hummingbird made camp,
And Crane ran on through the night.

Next morning, there he was, frying fish,
On the other side of the creek.
It didn't worry Hummingbird to see him there;
Soon he was out of sight. That night, though,
Crane passed him at midnight
While Hummingbird lay dreaming.
Next morning, when Hummingbird ran past,
Crane was done with breakfast, up and running.
Each day, a little gain:
The fourth day, Crane was catching dinner
When his rival passed.
At the end of the sixth day, Crane was ahead,
The whole night his to run alone.
Over the hill from the finish line
On the seventh morning,
Crane ate well, bathed, braided his hair,
And ran slowly to the mark, at the first light of dawn.
Hummingbird?
He crossed the line late in the afternoon.
Hot, sweaty, exhausted, defeated,
But he still looked good,
And acted better, ruefully praising his rival.
The girl? She broke her word, of course.
Crane was still homely, she said.
As he walked away his grandmother
Whispered something in his ear.
What was it? He never told,
But whatever it was, he smiled.
It wasn't a year after that we feasted at his wedding
To a girl whose eyes lit up
Whenever he looked at her.

KW
Tobacco

He couldn't see any sense to it.
Just because only those Southerners had the seed,
They traded tobacco only when they felt like it,
Sold it mixed with sticks and dirt sometimes,
Charged ten prices.
Hummingbird couldn't stand it.
It was time to go and *take* the seed,
He told the Council.
But the elders were alarmed;
No, they said, not worth going to war.
After each one had said the same thing,
Each in his own way,
"All it will take is one man," said Hummingbird.
(At this, the younger men traded wry glances.
They knew which "one man" he meant.)
In the end, they agreed, some of them hoping
This time Hummingbird might come home
Tail feathers dragging.
It was a long way, further than he thought,
Over tall mountain passes, pathless wilderness.
(Maybe those people
Weren't overcharging so much.)
But he kept going. Much as he hated
Worn-out moccasins, ragged clothes,
Cold camps, no one to talk to,
Doing things the hard way.
Finally he saw their village palisade from a hillcrest.
He crept closer.
No one at home
Would recognize handsome Hummingbird
In this bedraggled, muddy creature
Creeping through the underbrush to scout the way.
Well, he found the tobacco field all right:
Being men of sense, they had it guarded—

Night and day.
Hummingbird retreated, thought things over,
And munched on unripe berries for his dinner.
One thing was sure,
He wasn't going home without those seeds.
Call it false pride or not, he knew
Some of them would like it if he messed up,
Was just a bit embarrassed.
He'd take a risk to avoid that.
Well, he had to do something soon
Since he hadn't had a full meal in days.
A plan flashed into his mind,
The risky sort of thing he was always chided about.
He waited until twilight, not quite dark,
The time of day when you think you see
More than you do.
He crept up almost under the guard's feet,
Then, springing up, sprinted across the field,
Pulling the seeds without even breaking stride,
And away, like his namesake,
Before they got a good look.
Seconds later, safe in a hollow log,
He heard them searching and yelling.
He had a long, miserable walk home.
Most of the time, it rained.
But he really didn't mind
Walking into his village at sunset,
Barefoot, clothes mere scraps, dirty, sweaty, hungry,
And holding up for all to see
The pouch of tobacco seeds.

ᎫᎩᏟ ᎫᎤᏤᎢ ᏃᏛᏏ

Starfeathers

I never believed he was a prophet.
Not that I'm smarter than other people,
No, I'm just an ordinary guy,
Just that I knew Badger when we were boys.
He's not really such a bad fellow, exactly,
Just a little prone to do things the easy way,
To think he's the cleverest guy in the world.
He's got his good points—
Travelled everywhere, has Badger,
And he can tell a tale.
Well, he showed up in my town last summer,
And he wasn't too pleased to see me there.
I thought maybe he was up to something,
And at the next dance, there he was,
Appearing suddenly in the torchlight
In the strangest feather headdress.
It was purple and blue and green, all iridescent,
And he booms out in a loud, hollow voice,
"You see me here in feathers
From no bird on earth,"
And he flaps
This matching feather cape he's got on.
Everybody sucks in their breath.
"Starfeathers," he intones, "from the sky.
Hear my prophecy."
And everybody says, "Oooooh," except me.
He finishes up
Saying he's got to go back to the stars
So the spirits can tell him more stuff,
And he fades back, out of the light.
Well, somehow, I didn't believe the spirits
Were using old Badger for a mouthpiece,

No matter what he wore on his head.
But from then on, every time we had a dance
Or Council meeting at night,
Here comes Badger
With more words from the stars.
Funny thing, the stars always told us
To treat old Badger right.
By this time,
He'd moved in with a good-looking widow
And her even prettier daughter
And was eating very well,
And they'd started in called him the Messenger
And a bunch of other fancy names.
Well, I wondered
Why it was he only did prophecies at night,
And where did he keep his outfit
If it didn't go back to the stars?
Well, the next time he showed up
With the good word,
I noticed that he was *wet*!
I slipped out before he got finished,
And I followed him, right to the creek.
He plunged in—
To my surprise, he didn't come up again.
How did he do it? I pondered that one for days.
And then one morning it came to me.
I went to the creek, dived in, and swam
To the old beaver lodge's underwater entrance.
Now, what do you suppose I found?
Badger's Starfeather outfit.
That, and a waterproof bag.
I slipped around the village
And let the others know.
After our delegation called on Badger,
We weren't surprised he left town.

Now every time in the Council
Somebody starts in to act pompous,
One of us whispers, "Starfeathers."
It brings them back to earth,
For, it was told us by the trader,
Those Starfeathers
Come from a white man's barnyard fowl,
A symbol of vanity, he said.

ᎭᏍᏗ ᎠᏴ ᏏᏆᎸᏒ

Rabbit and Possum

Poor old Possum.
He never did have a lick of sense,
Even as a child, always running behind the others,
Never chosen first, too weak, too little,
Standing on the sidelines, grinning nervously,
Blinking his little eyes. No wonder
He thought it was so fine
To have Jack Rabbit for a friend.
Friend?
Fellows like Jack don't have friends, just dupes.
But nobody could tell Possum that:
He wouldn't listen.
Rabbit was full of schemes,
Mostly to prove how smart he was,
How dumb everybody else. Take the time
Jack noticed that half these village chiefs
Never went to Council, including his.
Too busy. Planting time, roof needing fixing,
Crops getting ripe, something.
So Jack went around telling everybody
He'd just come from Council
And the chiefs decided
Everybody had to make love,
Right now. Jack would be glad to help out.
(Well, *some* people fell for it.)
Of course, Possum grabbed for a girl
Just as everybody's grandmother
Arrived to break up the party
And break up
Whoever started such disreputable goings-on.
Jack Rabbit jumped out the window,
And ran away laughing.

Limping and bruised, Possum followed,
Getting to the next town
In time to hear Jack declare
The chiefs wanted everyone to fight.
He got knocked out, of course.
And after they brought him to,
Possum dragged himself on, to find
Jack had told the next town
Everybody had to get married,
But all the girls were taken,
So, again, Possum didn't get one.
Well, just then,
All those angry folks from the first town
Showed up. Jack Rabbit? Nowhere to be found.
But there stood Possum, asking plaintively
If there weren't some girl left over.
As they all pounced, Possum at last
Did something on his own: he fainted.
As he lay there with his eyes rolled up in his head,
The angry fathers, brothers, lovers, and husbands
Threw up their hands in disgust
And on second thought let him go.
No use talking to Possum.
Next time Rabbit's up to his old tricks,
There'll be Possum, trotting along behind him.
The only thing he learned from his close call was
When in trouble, pass out.

LOG
Tlanuwa

It may have been the breeze
From flower-starred meadows
That made me restless; all I know is
I had a sudden fancy for fresh meat for supper.
Coming through the grass up on the ridge
A shadow passed over me.
I thought it was a cloud, looked up—
And froze.
Floating overhead an enormous bird of prey:
Tlanuwa!
I thought, "But that's not real—a children's story . . ."
I dived, too late, for cover.
She stooped, she dived, she had me.
When she hit me I thought I was dead.
But no. She had me by the backpack
And, with the beating of powerful wings,
We rose—
Not without effort, mind you; a little faltering,
A few sudden, heart-stopping drops in altitude
Before she dropped me, sprawling, on a ledge.
I sat up cautiously, looked around,
And almost fainted.
The river, far, far below, looked like a ribbon,
The trees like bean bushes.
As I looked over that drop,
To the rocks below, that ledge seemed to shrink.
I swear my fingers almost dug into the solid rock!
It didn't help my swimming head one bit
For Tlanuwa to nudge me in the back,
Pushing me toward her large and sloppy nest.
"Stop that!" I screamed, "all right,
I'll sit in your nest, I'm going, I'm going!"

In the nest were her babies,
Two turkey-sized, nearly bald chicks,
The ugliest things in the world.
"What do you want me to do?" I yelled.
She threw a worm into one maw and nudged me.
I learn fast!
I started shoveling food into their mouths.
Behind me, I heard the sound of flapping wings,
Fading into the distance.
"She flies off,
And leaves me to take care of her kids," I said.
"Fine mother *that* is."
I had a lot to think about,
While the ugly twins napped.
How to escape, how to get down off that cliff,
How about dinner?
She returned at sunset, dragging a deer.
I got the haunch. It was great if you like raw meat.
(She got a little threatening over fires.)
Well, it was a very long and interesting summer.
I learned many things,
Some I'd just as soon not know.
But I never learned to like raw meat,
Heights, shrill, unexpected cries,
The smell of bird lime,
And dead worms at close quarters,
And I never got over the fear
Of rolling over in my sleep.
My charges got bigger every day,
And harder to wrestle
Back into their nests. They were still pretty ugly.
What was she going to do
When her toddlers no longer needed me?
I thought I'd rather not stay to find out.
I dragged one baby

To the edge, grabbed a foot, and shoved it off.
It flew a lot better than I thought.
"What I want is to land!" I yelled.
I reached up and smacked it on the head,
And, dazed, it descended.
I dropped off into a treetop and headed home.
"Bath, hot food, clean clothes, bath,
Solid ground!" I chanted.
Hey, you know what?
This whole thing's one crazy joke on me:
Now I've got a story even my *mother* won't believe!

୨୧୦
Frog

No one could please that old woman.
The fact is, she just didn't want that girl to marry,
At least, not then. She was the youngest,
Born long after the old folks
Thought they'd have another;
Sweet natured, she sang at her work all day,
And she could cook—
Oh, she could make anything
Taste good. But I must admit
I was asking where she lived
Before I knew all that
On looks alone.
Well, I'm not the best-looking fellow
In the Seven Towns,
But people don't set the dogs on me, either.
I work hard, and,
Though I'm not one of your famous warriors,
Nor the best hunter, my family wouldn't starve.
Her mother shouldn't have spoken to me like that.
She wouldn't even let me in the house.
If I had loved that girl less,
If she hadn't spoken,
I would never have crept back that night.
I heard my beautiful one crying in her bed.
I knelt among her mother's bean plants
All amazed.
A girl so lovely, and she cries for me?
Well, I surely don't deserve this, but now
I really have to do something, I told myself.
As I crouched there, plain old Frog,
I thought, "I'll show her 'frog.' "

I spent the day
Fixing up a dried gourd into a speaking trumpet,
And practicing where no one could hear me.
In the evening shadows,
When the old woman went for water,
I pitched my voice deep
And softly whispered into the gourd,
"Troublemaker, troublemaker, troublemaker."
She said, "What? Did someone speak?"
"Gonna croak, gonna croak, gonna croak!"
Well, I'd thought I made a pretty good frog of it
Practicing in the woods,
But she almost startled me
Into giving myself away.
She dropped her dipper
And ran screaming to the house.
It's a wonder her heart hadn't stopped altogether
(Except it was probably all dried up,
The old scoundrel.)
She thought she'd heard a Witch Frog after her,
And asked them all what it could mean.
And, bless them, all of them replied,
"It's an awful warning.
You'd better let her marry Frog!"
Well, she did. Even doing her own cooking
Was better than having to deal with a Witch Frog
Whenever she went to the spring.
And from then on,
She talked to me real nice, and edged away
As fast as she could.
Still, we talked it over, my wife and I,
And now we live in another town,
As far away as we can get.

ᏗᎾᏟ ᎠᏂᏆᎵᏏᎦ ᎠᏥ ᏔᎵ ᎠᎾᏓ ᏎᎦᎯᏔ

The Ball Game of
the Birds and the Animals

You think you've seen ball games?
Hey, they don't play real stickball nowadays,
Not like they used to play when I was young,
Not a bit!
Now the best game I ever saw back then,
It was a challenge match.
You've probably heard of it,
Only you haven't heard it right, not at all.
Why, they say it was between animals and birds,
Not men at all, but, listen to me, I was there!
It was this way:
Most of the fellows on the team that challenged
Had names like Deer and Tortoise,
Bear and Beaver,
So we *called* them the Animal Team, that's all.
The team they wanted to beat
Was called the Birds, same reason,
Never was a better team anywhere,
Overhill or Underhill, than them,
And, like I say, never was a better game.
This fellow Bear was captain of the Animal Team;
Didn't have much speed,
But he was sure powerful.
You know, he could pick up any man on his team,
And not even gasp for breath.
Deer was the fast one, Terrapin
Could outlast all the rest—
Play all day and dance all night.
Now Eagle was captain of the Birds.
He was both strong and fast,
Never saw a big man move so fast.

But their speediest man was Hawk,
Their strong man Tlanuwa.
Only man I ever heard of called that,
And, come to think of it,
Only man I ever saw come close to earning it.
All those fellows were good, and good *folks*, too.
Well, before the game started,
Here come two little fellows over to talk to Eagle.
They were from the Animal Team's village,
But Bear'd turned them down for his team—
Said they were too lightweight.
Well, Eagle was a kindhearted fellow,
And he had the sort of attitude toward ball games
You seldom see nowadays.
(Well, it wasn't all that common then, either.)
He told them they had the heart to play,
And what's a game for,
But playing the best you can,
Not just seeing who scores!
Well, Eagle and those fellows
Liked being called the Birds so much
They took a fancy
To give the new men names to match,
And, since they should really
Have been on the Animal Team,
They called them Tlameha, Bat,
And Tewa, Flying Squirrel,
And felt they were real clever.
They commenced to practice then,
And, when they threw the ball to Bat,
Saw him dodge and circle with it,
Never letting it drop,
They knew he'd be fine.
Well, when they tried out Tewa,
He was pretty good, too. Sure was!

You should have seen his jumps!
All of them laughed then,
Mighty pleased with themselves
For giving their new teammates
Just the right names,
And getting two good players on the team.
At the signal to start, there goes Tewa,
Almost the instant of the toss,
He's got the ball, he passes it to Eagle,
And the rest keep it in the air for a great, long play;
When the ball finally drops,
Here's Martin racing Bear,
But Bat beats them both,
And down the field he goes,
Dodging and dancing, doubling and darting—
I tell you even Deer couldn't catch him—
And it was Bat who scored.
All that bragging,
And Bear and Terrapin
Didn't touch a finger to that ball.
Well, now you've heard how it really was,
And I'm telling you, I was there!
Why, how do you suppose I ever got myself
A funny name like Flying Squirrel?
Yes, Great-Grandson, it was me, it really was.
A long time ago, long time,
But you never saw a better ball game—
Why, people are talking about it yet.

ᏅᏓᏇᎯ ᎠᏧᏥ
Lazy Boy

It was amazing how that boy hated to work.
He was his mother's darling, true,
But he was lazy
Before she started making excuses for him.
Nobody quite knew why—
None of the rest of the family was like that.
Maybe he was born that way, they said.
Well, finally, his old granny
Caught him watching ants
When he should have been hoeing.
It wasn't that he liked ants so much;
It was just that he could watch them lying down.
"I wish I was an ant," he said, sulking.
"They *never* have to hoe the garden."
("Should I or shouldn't I?" she thought.
"Oh, why not?")
ZAP!
He was an ant
Surrounded by thirty bigger ants
Yelling at him in ant language
To pick up a crumb of cornbread
The size of a large boulder,
And here came enemy ants, screaming harshly,
Waving and clicking huge, sharp pincers.
"Granny!" he screamed.
He hoed corn all that day,
Without complaint, in the hot sun.
It didn't last.
Next day they were gathering wood.
Now where was he?
Asleep, under a tree.
Awakened rudely, he complained,
"Wish I was a tree."

And there he was, whipping in the wind,
His roots all parched with drought,
Shaken for nuts until his boughs rattled,
Threatened with an ax.
"Oh, no!" he screamed.
His mother didn't have to ask him twice
To get her water
For a while.
But he got tired of it again.
Out came that lower lip.
"Scrubbing pots, hauling water.
Wish I was a deer."
WHAM! And zzzzip, an arrow nearly got him.
He bolted into the forest. In the dusk,
He stood trembling and exhausted by a brook.
Just as he bent to drink, he heard a panther.
"Oh, please," he begged.
He was a boy again for weeks and weeks.
He even worked,
Until the day
His father and brothers were building a fish trap.
He hated hauling stones, standing in cold water;
He got so tired.
"Rocks don't have to work.
Wish I was a rock," he muttered.
ZING! He was a rock. He really liked it.
No heavy lifting, scrubbing, sweating.
And nothing much bothers rocks, he thought.
Clink! Clink!
"Somebody's *banging* on me!
They *chipped* me! Help!"
It was a warrior, making arrowheads.
Well, back to being a boy again,
And here came Granny, carrying honey cakes.
"Well," he said, "there are good points
In being a boy, I guess."

ᏍᏆᏗᏄ

Hunter

Everybody knew he was lazy,
Shiftless and lazy.
Quatie thought she was insulted
When he started hanging around her door.
"What do I want with you?" she said.
"I can grow corn and beans on my own,
And if I wanted to eat lizards,
I could catch them by myself as well.
Go on home. I'll either marry a good hunter
Or stay single all my life."
Well, he took her seriously,
But he wasn't planning on working—
That wasn't in him to do.
A few months later, though, he shot a deer.
(How? Even a deer can have an off day.)
Of course, he remembered pretty Quatie,
And maybe even her fine, well-kept cornfield
That could feed him the rest of his life;
He put that deer over his shoulder,
And, singing loudly,
Walked down the trail past her house.
She and her mother were out pulling weeds.
(Goodness, how hard those women worked,
And in the hot sun, too!)
He waved and smiled.
As soon as he was out of sight, he doubled back,
Dropped the deer, and took a little nap.
A few hours later, back down the trail he came,
Deer hoisted up on his shoulder,
Waving and smiling.
He did it again, about sunset. This time,
Quatie waved back.

For three days, he did the same thing—
He was wearing the hair off that deer.
"Quatie," said her mother,
"Could it be that folks are mistaken?
He might just have been bashful or modest."
Well, that evening, by chance,
She decided to go for a little walk.
And while she was out, she thought
She'd call on that young man's mother.
"Your son certainly has turned out well."
—"How can you say that?
He's the laziest fellow in town."
"But he's brought back three deer
Every day this week!"
—"He's brought back *no* deer this week."
"I've seen him coming by my house with them."
—"I tell you, he's never brought them home!"
What was all this?
She told the whole thing to her husband,
Who backtracked the lazy young man.
There, in the brush, was his cache:
One deer carcass, thoroughly rotten.
The funny part, they all concluded,
Was that the lazy young man
Had probably worked harder being tricky
Than most fellows do when they work.

ᏉᏫ ᎠᏍᎦᏎᏫ ᎩᎦᏗ

Thunder's Sister

You know all those stories that say
"Leave strange women alone."?
I should have listened. But how could I think of it
While looking at a beautiful girl?
Especially one like her. Her hair
Was enough to rivet my attention. It was so long,
So glossy and thick. I got someone to speak to her.
Yes, right there, I was ready to be her husband.
Well, her reply was, "I have to ask my brother."
And while I waited, I must fast for seven days.
Sure. Anything. I was game.
Well, seven days later,
There she was, her and her sister,
And at daylight, we set out, leaving the dance.
They led the way,
First down a trail I'd never seen before—
And this was *my* village! Reaching the creek,
They stepped out on the water.
"No," I said, "I can't walk on water."
"This isn't water," they replied,
"This is the trail home."
And I stepped forth.
(It was only grass, only the trail, I told myself.)
We came to the river, the wide and deep Tallulah.
"I can't go on; I'll drown," I cried.
"It's the main trail, that's all it is," came the reply.
(Yes, it's the main trail, I told myself; go on.)
We came to a cave right under Ugunyi,
Tallulah Falls.
They went inside, and there I stood.
"Come in," they called.
"Why are you standing before the door?"

(It is the house, I told myself;
That is the roof, the walls.)
But then at the door, they paused,
Took off their shawls,
Then took off their hair, hanging it up on pegs.
"Oh, sit by me," my bride said. "Here's a chair."
"It's a turtle," I said,
As it stretched its claws and snapped.
"It's a chair," she said firmly,
Her bald head gleaming.
(Chair, chair, I told myself.)
"Oh, I hear our brother coming!" she said.
Well, Brother asked me to take a ride,
And asked them to fetch a horse.
"That's the biggest snake in the world," I said.
"It's a horse," he said.
"A horse." "A horse," they echoed.
(That snake is actually a horse, I told myself.)
"Oh, give him a bracelet; a necklace or two;
He'll feel better about it then," he said.
They were living, scaly snakes,
Twisting about my arms, my neck.
"What kind of place is this!" I screamed.
"I can't live here!"
"Coward!" snarled the brother,
Striking me senseless.
Well, he can call me names if he wants to;
I don't care if he's right. All I know is,
I don't want to walk on water,
Live in a cave under a waterfall,
Ride on snakes and sit on turtles,
Wear a water snake as a bracelet, but most of all,
I'm not going to make love to a bald-headed girl,
No matter *whose* sister she is!

ᏣᎳᎩᎭᏃᏓ ᎠᏴ
The Girl Who
Couldn't Cook Soup

You listen to me: I *know* how to make kanuche.
First you pound the hickory nuts, shells and all;
Then you roll the shells and meat
Into fist-sized balls;
You dry them all winter,
Then you throw them into a pot of stock,
Add hominy, and,
When it's well cooked, dish it out.
You see? I know.
The truth of it is,
He didn't really want to get married.
It was all his father's idea.
How could I know?
He came to our town for a ball game.
You should have seen him, golden in the sun;
All the girls
Watched him with their mouths hanging open,
Not just me.
He asked the other guys who I was
(My cousin told me),
And he came to talk to my family.
I believed him.
He just seemed the sort of fellow
To court a girl like that.
Anyway, he *was* good looking, and insistent,
and we married.
And I went with him
Back to his old father who was all alone—
Yes, I was even willing
To leave my town and my family.
He ran ahead and burst into the house;

"Father, Father, I've done it!" he cried,
"I've brought you back a bride!"
(What's this, I thought,
Brought *Father* back a bride?)
"Now you won't have to eat my cooking,
Or even worse, your own, as we've been doing
Since your old woman died."
As I stood there rooted in my tracks,
The old man turned to me.
"Better get dinner started, wife of my son,
Before you hoe the corn," he said.
Now wasn't *that* a welcome?
Well, I just hung my packs in the corner
And started cleaning house.
(She couldn't have been much of a housewife,
Or else she'd been dead for several years.)
You never saw such a mess: old fishbones
Thrown on the floor, mildew everywhere, trash.
Their clothes—I threw away more than I mended,
And then searched an hour for a pan.
Where were *they*? Went fishing, the both of them,
The minute I reached for the broom.
While I heated the water,
I thought. Supper!
That was my inspiration! It truly was.
You should have seen their expressions
When I went to dish out the kanuche
And whole hickory nuts splashed in the bowls.
"What? Where's the kanuche balls?" they said.
Didn't I know enough even to crack the nuts?
(Oh, the identical horrified looks of their faces.)
Well, we agreed to end the marriage.
The boy took me sorrowfully home.
"Teach her to cook!" he shouted to my mother
When he got a safe distance from the house.

But that isn't all. The pair of them
Are busily proving the old adage
That men gossip worse than women.
Thanks to them,
I'm now known in the Seven Towns
As the girl who can't even cook soup!

ᏉᎵ
Kanuche

My pop always says,
"These young girls we got nowadays
Don't hardly know how to start bein' a woman."
And he's right, Pops is!
I guess maybe you're going to say
I'm just soured on women
On account of what happened to me,
But it ain't *my* doing!
You must've heard I went and got married.
Three weeks ago and I'm still mad—
And the whole town's still laughing.
Didn't even last all day.
She was back at her mother's before the sun set.
Well, you know Pops and me,
We been trying to do for ourselves
Since Quail—that was his last old woman—
Just up and keeled over and died on him one day.
Neither one of us can cook a lick,
And I ain't goin' to clean up his mess
Any more'n he's goin' to clean up mine.
We got kind of sick of it, living like that,
So I says to him,
"Pop, don't you think you ought to go courtin'?
Find you some nice widow-lady
With a good corn patch
And a light hand at making corn cakes.
Sure would be nice to get my shirts mended
And some real good dinners."
He says, "I'm old and wore out, Son.
It's strenuous courting women,
Minding your manners,
Talking nice to their mothers,

Watching out for their brothers—
Why, real good-looking ones gets all insulted
That you even showed a interest
If they don't like you!
I've done been married four times now.
I've done my part; it's your turn."
I tried to tell him
I'd caught him a couple of them women
By looking cuddly—
Something about a tearful orphan boy
That needs a hug
A woman who can cook just can't resist—
But, no, he wouldn't listen.
Well, I tried all the girls in town,
Even the ugly ones.
They just laughed.
"All you want is somebody
To clean out that old bear's cave
You call a house,
And cook for you and your pop."
So I happened to go over to Old Chota
For a ball game,
And I happened
To see this girl on the sidelines watching.
Good night, she was good looking! In that crowd
She looked like a lily among dandelions.
So I asked about her, of course,
I went to her house, I courted her fast and hard,
But I forgot to find out could she cook.
I sweet-talked her
Into coming back to Pop with me
After we married, instead of my moving to Chota,
But was I sorry!
When she saw the mess in our house,
She clouded up like a thunderstorm;

She *did* start in to work, I'll say that for her;
Dust flew everywhere.
Pops and me, we went fishing.
When we come back, she'd got supper.
Smelled pretty good;
We hadn't had kanuche in a while, I can tell you,
But when she went to serve it—clunk, clunk,
Whole hickory nuts fell in the bowls,
Splashing hot soup all over us.
She didn't know
To crack the nuts before you cook 'em.
She'd tried to make kanuche—
Which any six-year-old can cook—
But *she* didn't use kanuche balls.
Well, that was that. We agreed to break up;
I took her home. And you know what else?
She cleaned up everything, even the yard;
It looked real good for a day or two,
But I'm still looking for about half my stuff.
These girls nowadays!
I may *never* get married.

Appendix

I recommend visiting Oconaluftee Indian Village in Cherokee, North Carolina, and Tsa-la-gi Ancient Village at the Cherokee Heritage Center in Tahlequah, Oklahoma. Both were created and are run by the Cherokee people, and both give visitors the chance to see and understand a way of life which no book and no museum exhibit can fully describe or explain.

The Smoky Mountain site of Oconaluftee is itself an aid to understanding Cherokee traditions. The village is set among tall trees and is threaded by small streams which tumble down a hillside. Local people demonstrate traditional arts and skills such as pottery making and blowgun shooting.

Tsa-la-gi Ancient Village is the re-creation of a Cherokee village of three hundred years ago, palisades, fish ponds, and all. It is populated by deerskin-clad local people who carry out daily life as if tourists and their guides are invisible; children swim in the pond, men make arrows and blowgun darts and construct wattle-and-daub houses, women cook and do chores, and villagers converse in Cherokee. It is from Tsa-la-gi Ancient Village that I have drawn much of my description of village life in the old days.

Near each village is a museum run by the Eastern Band of the Cherokee Indians and by the Cherokee Nation, respectively. Both museums display artifacts not to be seen elsewhere, exhibits which show Cherokee history, and contemporary art. Both use lively multimedia displays. The Museum of the Cherokee Indians in Cherokee, North Carolina, contains displays featuring traditional stories.

Cherokee, North Carolina, is located on U.S. 19 east of Bryson City and west of Asheville. Cherokee Heritage Center, the location of Tsa-la-gi Ancient Village, is in Tahlequah, Oklahoma, which is between Tulsa and Fort Smith, Arkansas.

The easiest way to drive there from the west is to take U.S. 62 from Muskogee, Oklahoma, to Fort Gibson and Tahlequah. The best route from Fort Smith is U.S. 40 to Vian, Oklahoma, then north to Tahlequah on Oklahoma 82. There are many areas near both sites for camping. There are camping areas in the Cherokee Reservation and throughout the Smoky Mountains and around Tenkiller Lake near Tahlequah.

Glossary

Above Ones   The Creator-God and all benevolent spiritual entities.

Ball game   Stickball was a traditional game similar to hockey, played on a grassy field the approximate size of a football field. Players used sticks to move the ball to the goals at either end of the field. People of all ages and both sexes played, and teams were of any size.

Conjuration, conjurors   Knowledge and use of magical or spiritual power was theoretically possible for anyone. Formulas—quick, highly abbreviated sequences of familiar thoughts, attitudes, and concepts used to produce magical results—were a custom as far back as the introduction of the Cherokee syllabary. Magic was traditionally divided into two parts: *saying* things and *doing* things. Those who practiced it were divided into two categories: those who cured and those who interfered. Maneuvering objects and altering physical states of being were seen as potentially dangerous. Conjuring implied seeking after dangerous power in order to manipulate others or to cause harm, so that calling someone a conjuror had a negative connotation, suggesting the practice of evil witchcraft.

Council   Village or tribal government.

Council House	The public meeting place designed for Council meetings was also used for any other large indoor gatherings. Traditionally, it had seven sides and seven rows of seats for the Seven Clans.
Dance arbor	The dancing or stomping ground near the village included an outdoor arena for dancing and ceremonies and surrounding benches for spectators. It was roofed by a sunscreen consisting of a permanent framework freshly thatched with pleasant-scented branches (usually cedar) before each use.
Elders	It was the custom for the old people in a community to act as an informal medical advisory board and to be consulted as repositories of knowledge. This was not a formalized activity; I have adopted terms like "elders" to highlight this commonly accepted behavior of asking old people for advice or information when a problem occurred.
Green Corn Dance	The ceremony marking rebirth and new beginnings was similar to New Year's as celebrated by people of European descent—resolutions were made and special food was served. The dance arbor was cleaned. People bathed ceremonially and put on new or clean clothes. All slights, quarrels, and offenses, even serious ones, were forgiven and forgotten. Household fires were extinguished and ceremonially relighted, and houses were cleaned from top to bottom.

Hunters	Mythic spirits who lived underwater and ate human flesh.
Immortals	The Nunnehi, or the People Who Live Anywhere, were benevolent, mythic spirits. Whenever and wherever they chose to appear, they looked and acted exactly like people. Their singing and dancing was of unearthly beauty and could be heard in strange, isolated places. The Nunnehi liked wild scenery and high elevations. They were kindly and sympathetic, often caring for lost people. They had a special concern for people fighting to defend their homes.
Kanati	Selu's husband was the mythic father of mankind and the bringer of hunting and woodlore to the people.
Kanuche	The traditional thick soup was made from broth, hominy, and kanuche balls, which were pounded hickory nuts rolled into balls and dried for several months.
Little Men	Small in stature, humanoid in appearance, these mythic beings were amoral. According to legend, they occupied the earth before Indians were created. They could and did assist people, but they were dangerous and could do harm, particularly through their rather malicious sense of humor.
Nightland	It was thought that the Darkened Land, or the Land of Death, could be reached by travelling westward.

Nunnehi	*See* Immortals.
Old ones	*See* Elders.
Overhill	The area that is now eastern Tennessee.
Powers	*See* Above Ones.
Quatie	Personal, female name of unknown origin, translated as Pretty or Darling.
Raven Leader	The title of the commanding officer of a military unit was also applied to the point-man, so that the leading position in the unit was also called Raven. Leading flankers and rear guards were given designations such as Fox and Owl.
Raven Mockers	Certain people used magical power to prolong their own lives through stealing the remainder of other people's lives. Killing Raven Mockers was considered perfectly moral. *See also* Conjuration, conjurors.
Red Chief	The man who ran affairs outside the village or nation was a combination secretary of defense, chairman of the Joint Chiefs of Staff, secretary of state, and chief negotiator of foreign trade. His opposite number, the White Chief, conducted all internal affairs. Chief judicial and law enforcement officer, the White Chief was also in charge of public works and sanitation.
Selu	The name commonly used for corn here refers to the Corn Mother, the mythic person who gave agriculture to the people and who was regarded as the primal ancestress of mankind.

Seven Towns	Seven was a special number; in this use, it simply meant "All over that part of the country."
Tewa	Personal name, usually male, translated as Flying Squirrel.
Thunder	The Red Man was a powerful, personalized spiritual entity, usually considered an aspect or embodiment of the Creator-God.
Tlameha	Personal name, usually male, translated as Bat.
Tlanuwa	There are a number of stories about this mythic, gigantic bird of prey.
Tuya	The name commonly used for beans was also a personal name, usually male.
Uk'ten'	This gigantic man-eating snake was said to lurk in deep water. Traditionally, both Uk'ten' and rattlesnakes were either people who had changed their shape or the descendants of such people; once changed, these conjurors either would not or could not change back.
Underhill	The area that is now northern Georgia.
Whippoorwill, Brown	This bird was regarded as a messenger of the spirits or a guardian spirit that helped people in need.
Wise ones	*See* Elders.
Yona	Personal name, usually male, translated as Bear.

Bibliography

Kilpatrick, Jack F. and Anna Gritts. *Friends of Thunder: Folktales of the Oklahoma Cherokees*. Dallas, Texas: Southern Methodist University Press, 1964.

Mooney, James. *Myths of the Cherokee*. Washington, D.C.: Bureau of American Ethnology, 1900.

West, C.W. "Dub." *Legends and Folklore of the Cherokees*. Muskogee, Oklahoma: Muskogee Publishing Company, 1980.

Books by Cherokee authors recommended for further reading:

Kilpatrick, Jack F. and Anna Gritts. *Run toward the Nightland: Magic of the Oklahoma Cherokees*. Dallas, Texas: Southern Methodist University Press, 1967.

————. *Walk in Your Soul: Love Incantations of the Oklahoma Cherokees*. Dallas, Texas: Southern Methodist University Press, 1965.

Strickland, Rennard. *Fire and the Spirits: Cherokee Law from Clan to Courts*. Norman, Oklahoma: University of Oklahoma Press, 1975.